THE PORTAGE POETRY SERIES

Praise for

The Watching Sky

"Even though these poems are accessible, grounded in both history and geography of place, and steer clear of prosodic calisthenics, they do not presume to think or feel for their readers. There is an open-endedness in both form and content, and a longing for something not quite attained that carries through to the final poem."

—Terry Lucas
author of *The Thing Itself*

"An authentic voice that makes us all believers. And the breath-grabbing emotionality never tastes saccharine. Rather it's as familiar as the desire we can never shake: to enter a warm home, following a dog with its leash, trailing."

—Lynne Thompson
author of *Fretwork*

"In *The Watching Sky*, Judy Brackett Crowe examines beauty in the face of mortality, and the sacred imprint of sensory memories. She explores what exists between tangible and abstract with poetic candor: '...she found herself in that cloud-shaped/map again, the colorful world still smelling/ of crayon and cedar, of onions and summer.' The poems are full of familiarity, dreaminess, and nostalgia for stories and the myths of common lives. It's Crowe's authentic details that deliver striking vibrancy: '...hair and needles, bark and fur, hooves and arms,/all suspended in ethereal light like floating/constellations, like the end and the beginning.'"

—Kirsten Casey
author of *Ex Vivo (out of the living body)*
Nevada County (CA) Poet Laureate

"In *The Watching Sky*, landscapes of mind and exterior realities come to life, urban and rural, peopled with often charming populations, such as the storytellers from Ms. Crowe's rural upbringing who have left tales dangling, tantalizing us with the ongoing task poets must take up. The spectrum that unfolds here is ambitious in the best sense—from childhood, family, society, and mankind's effect on the natural world that includes its greedy and suicidal tromping over the human soul and our most sensitive selves. In this sense the poet has not given up. She stands against the dulling and dumbing down of the world for the life that's in us and around us. So it is an embattled voice that rings out in the book, a challenge to feel and act with awareness and delight."

—Gene Berson
author of *Raveling Travel*

"In *The Watching Sky*, we stroll through Judy Brackett Crowe's poems like the landscapes of her 'immense, cloud-shaped world,' in awe of what is noticed and captured in every rich detail of Earth's beautifully relentless lessons on life and death, shadow and light, and where we find home. Whether it is in reflections of 'cello sounds and jasmine air,' a little girl hopscotching all the way home, of once being a bird 'when the world was young...,' or even beyond the sky into the 'fall-off places' that are full of burning wonder— over each creek and mountain, and under every moon-washed sky, we revel in Crowe's exquisite affirmations of finding home in nature's every wingbeat."

—Julie Valin
author of *Songs for Ghosts*

THE WATCHING SKY

poems

Judy Brackett Crowe

CORNERSTONE PRESS
UNIVERSITY OF WISCONSIN-STEVENS POINT

Cornerstone Press, Stevens Point, Wisconsin 54481
Copyright © 2024 Judy Brackett Crowe
www.uwsp.edu/cornerstone

Printed in the United States of America by
Point Print and Design Studio, Stevens Point, Wisconsin

Library of Congress Control Number: 2023950493
ISBN: 978-1-960329-31-8

Cornerstone Press titles are produced in courses and internships offered by the
Department of English at the University of Wisconsin–Stevens Point.

DIRECTOR & PUBLISHER
Dr. Ross K. Tangedal

EXECUTIVE EDITORS
Jeff Snowbarger, Freesia McKee

EDITORIAL DIRECTOR
Ellie Atkinson

SENIOR EDITORS
Brett Hill, Grace Dahl

PRESS STAFF
Lily Alsteen, Carolyn Czerwinski, Chloe Cieszynski, Kirsten Faulkner, Sophie
McPherson, Natalie Reiter, Lauren Rudesill, Anthony Thiel, Ava Willett

For
Jeanne-Marie & Don, Esther Rose, Quinn
Jonathan & Christi, Finnegan
Matthew, Jack & Brie, Sam

Also by Judy Brackett Crowe:

Flat Water: Nebraska Poems

POEMS

— SHE —

— WORDS AND PICTURES, SONG —

— WHAT MATTERS —

SHE

While She's Thinking About Weeks of Bad News

This sunny/rainy day is not enough
to slake her thirst   for calm, for grace,
yet she says thanks   anyway

for water, for lime zest, for white-tailed brown bird
          that flies into the glass   lands stunned
and unblinking for lightning-flash moments

then lifts and wings, wobbly,
to porch rail   to oak branch   to gone.

Flight Plan

Bone blades jut where her wings were once
affixed. Rolling her shoulders back and down,
she can feel the pulse, the strength of them,
can almost remember flying.

Riding the bike down the steep and winding
pot-holed lane—airborne, almost. Swinging
on the old saddle hanging from the rafters
in the hayloft—hay bales stacked

against the walls, mice nests, bird nests, barn
cats prowling, the owl tucked into his high-up
corner, haydust motes fogging the air,
she sneezing and swinging—no horse,

just girl and saddle, the barn window thrown
open to the green world, she wondering
if she can swing high enough, fast enough,
far enough, swim/fly out the window and dive

into the pond or the house-high haystack.
No, not the haystack—needles, errant pitchforks.

Inside a Pearl

She swallows the pearl   uncultured it is
so is she   inside the pearl
sleeps mustard seed or
                a babe's clipped nail or
a kitten's eyelash or
                something else alive and
spinning warm
          she walks toward
the far distant middleness
with a pebble in
her shoe   she put it there
to remember   always
that she's of this earth
                not of the air
she cannot fly   doesn't want
to fly   all that air swishing
as she swings ever higher
toward the moon
tonight barely one night
past full
      she swallows the moon
                nor of the water
she cannot swim   such effort
to stay afloat   part of her wanting
to be vertical
      in
      water
she walks on
thinking she must be glowing
willing the pearl
the pebble
the spinning night
to save her.

Questions for *Quercus Lobata*

Is she dreaming this life or some other
life, or has she slipped into someone else's
dream or daydream or nightmare
and if "our little lives are rounded with a sleep"—
or is it "rounded with sheep"—
   (*sheep-surround?*—nothing scarier than a herd
   of dead-eyed sheep, bumper-sheeping
   munching grasses, forbs, legumes)
and she wonders—are there dreams at both ends
of the "round"
   (not that rounds have ends)
and while she's in and out of dreamtime, ruminating
   (those pesky sheep slipping in here again)
she ponders the odd plurals—
deer fish moose pike swine sheep et cetera
but can't discern anything in common
among those species to grant them special plural status
   (except—each one has two eyes
   some have gills, some hooves)
and now she's a little worried about the shepherd boy fast
asleep under the haystack
   (as opposed to *slow asleep*—how does that work?)
and wonders whether sheep dream
   (dogs do, for sure, the border collie asleep on his rug
   dream-worrying about a lost little lamb, whimpering
   legs pedaling)
and thinks a woolly-herd collective dream is more likely
   (i.e., the sheep are so, well, *sheeplike*, they
   might not know how to have their own dreams)—
   a simple dream of hard-working, eagle-eyed
   white-tail-flag collie's snarls and nips, a shepherd's crook—
and leads her to wonder whether the eagle dreams, decides
probably not, it's just too focused, its eyes bigger than
its brain, no room for dreams

                                       so—do the eyes have it?
(e)yes, they do, the two-lobed soul lodged not in some heart
chamber or gastro pocket, though perhaps in that tender wrist spot
blue vein pulsing

                      and in her startled, full awakening, she finds
no answers, just dogs and sheep, birds and words, and tufts
of wool clinging to the branches of a dying valley oak
in the center of a pasture along Lakeville Road, a hieroglyph
silhouette against the dusky sky
living for hundreds of years
dying for hundreds of years

                                       but—how
do sleep and sheep and shepherd boy
and dog and dream and dying oak
(the galls of the oak its blind eyes?)
account for earthquakes ringing church bells
sending dogs to tremble, to scurry, while sheep
stare skyward, unblinking, unperturbed?

Geography of a Cloud

Once on a long-ago winter's day she drew
a huge map of her world on butcher paper,
using every crayon stub in the small
cedar box that held the bright clear colors
of her life, an immense cloud-shaped world,
endless, with hills and wide rivers,
stick people, kind people like Teacher
and her aunties and her friend Jane,
houses, horses, dogs, sunflowers
and hollyhocks. The torn blue edges
were the sky and whatever lived beyond
the fall-off places and beyond the sky—
roiling deserts, flat black seas, ice-bound
lands—triangle creatures with wiry whiskers
and many legs.

Later, hundreds of thousands of miles later,
bittersweet and periwinkle and Prussian blue
and flesh and magenta later, and thistle, salmon,
gold and silver later, after decades in the fall-off
places, she found herself in that cloud-shaped
map again, the colorful world still smelling
of crayon and cedar, of onions and summer,
and of the fields she'd looked down upon
from her childhood window in that long-ago
time, surprised to find her map so small
and so red, blue, and yellow strange.

Night Travelers

Firefly and night lily bring flickering
faux sunlight, but soon the world goes dark.

Isn't it odd that they whose day is night
wake in the gloom to inconstant moon
or starshine or stygian skies,
no rising-in-the-east rosy fingers
stroking their eyelids, warming their faces.
Those big-eyed, color-blind, nearsighted ones—
bat, fox, owl, opossum, raccoon, skunk, scorpion—
hunt and travel through our sleep,
ears and noses searching for food.

In the desert, a bat dives into the milky bowl
of a night-blooming cereus, lapping up nectar
and bearing pollen to the next bloom until,
sated and near drunk with sustenance and delight,
he steers back to the roost and settles
downside up, wings tucked.

The non-winged night owl, alone on the lawn,
her eyes reconciling with the dark, watches
the red fox slinking along the fence and listens
to the *whoo-hoo-hoo* of the great horned owl
in the sugar maple. The fox gives a harsh bark.
The owl swoops down, so close she can feel
its wingbeats. A wisp of damp rises from the grass,
and she is swathed in a musky, fruity, foreign smell.

She thinks of the desert—
brown, baked air,
miles of sand and sun,
months with no rain.

Lower Mathematics

The little boy shouts "To infinity and beyond!"
and asks "Where the heck is infinity?"
and "Is a googol bigger than a gazillion?"
and "How can there be a biggest number?
Doesn't the whole entire world have room

for 1 or 2 or 3 more?"
and "How can there be something littler than zero?"
She tells him—snowflakes, grains of sand, chess
moves, broken promises, teardrops and raindrops,
stars and universes, seeds in dandelion puffs

floating in a summer breeze.
He closes his eyes. "I'm trying to see a gazillion
gazelles!" She wonders how math people can talk
to each other when they can't even agree
on whether a billion is a million millions

or a thousand millions. "False friends," they say.
She closes her eyes and sees—tears
flowing over broken promises,
becoming part of the air,
drizzling back up into the clouds,

and showering down again next January
in a googol's worth of raindrops—
plus 1 or 2 or 3.
She doesn't know what to tell the boy
about zero.

The Weight of Silence

The house is nearly empty now except for plants
and dust and her. The avocado tree (ten years ago
a tooth-picked seed) climbs ceilingward.

The leaves of the figless ficus stretch wide.
In this green room she steps around the border
of the Nepali rug with lambs and children playing

on the grassy banks. Her life indoors and out
of doors is much the same, though bentwood chairs
seem out of place out back in her forsaken field

of sun and ruts and rocks, the only live thing there
blue chicory. She remembers cello sounds
and jasmine air and waves dying on the sands
in Monterey. She remembers saying to her children,

"Mira mar." The weight of silence breaks
when jays and crows agree to disagree or when
in these dry, hot, endless days she hears sirens

and the *whop whop whop* of helicopters flying
to or from the river, to or from yet another
swimmer in deep distress. In the long evenings,
she feels this place alive with animals and children.

The Year of Living Nervously

1963

The year she had the breakdown
things were going to hell
in a handbasket
so many things   small and big
anonymous bad guys   Little Red's wolf
Ấp Bắc   Gò Công
and more
You could call it the Inferno Basket
spilling smells
    overheating engines
    woodsmoke
    prairie burn

So   in the frayed quilted pouch
she wore everywhere
she put treasures   and hopes
        4 little Birmingham girls
            growing older   playing in the side yards
            their ankles dusty   their skirts dancing
        122 boys' next birthdays
        the president's plane trip canceled
        Meyer lemons
        spicebush seedpods
        crusty blue-white snow
        a baby on the way

Reading the Night

She can't hear them falling,
the leaves, the middle-of-the-night
falling leaves—
the oaks, the maples, the liquidambars—
as, sleepless, she reads
30 or 40 or 100 pages of some
new novel she'll remember none of
come next read,

but a low far-off sound—
not leaves, not fox, not coyote—
pulls her for a moment and she sees
one perfect leafhand swirling
through an October window and settling
on the O-mouth of an old man,
book tenting on his chest
and the leaf not moving,
slowly reddening there,
drying and shrinking there

for days, and during the next
middle-of-the-night, wide-awake time,
she'll leaf through her book, searching
for the old man, for the perfect
red leaf.

Dreaming Awake

She wakes up dreaming, goes through the day somewhere
else, traipses through sleet and wind, cold sun now
and then, climbs up scree slopes,
over and around lichen-painted boulders
skyward to the saint's aerie,
sheep and dogs musical notes
in the fields far below

      spreads cardboard, leaves, woodchips
      between the berry rows
      hint of berry scent in the breeze
      not really but there will be come August

walks the circuit from his alleged birthplace in town,
low ceilings, heavy timbers, to Mary Arden's farm,
thatched roofs, brisk day, school children taking notes,
eating lunch—maybe that clever boy ran in these
his grandfather's fields, maybe not

      washes the windows of winter's grime
      white vinegar crumpled newspaper
      back and forth outside and in
      wiping off damned spots

wades through high grasslands, waves away flies
and a black-haired boy on horseback who pleads,
"Come along, I can show you a cavern.
My father makes fine caps,"
plucks a bloody eagle feather from a sprig of edelweiss

      turns pages eyes skimming words
      through memory's fog
      can't remember what she's read
      reads page nine
      nine times

watches a small, tan, one-legged bird hopping
on the deck, beaking crumbs and tweedling
as the waves roll in, frangipani in the air

      chops onions crushes garlic scrubs carrots
      and blue potatoes flattens chicken breasts
      sprinkles herbs splashes white wine

wends her way up and around the squares and circles,
Borobudur temple, not praying exactly,
Merapi bubbling in the hazy distance,
Buddhas on pedestals, in niches everywhere,
peeks into a beehive stone-windowed stupa—
scores of sun-dappled Buddhas in shifting light,
stumbles upon a stone garden of Buddha parts,
hands and feet, takes photos and thinks
about form, formlessness, desire

      collects kindling picks the last
      berries the last
      green tomatoes
      gathers the first
      fallen linden leaves, hearts
      and the first
      fallen maple leaves, hands

eats Indian food takeout in musty Hereford B&B,
breakfast of tomatoes, beans, triangles of toast,
New Year's Day morning, one child not there,
follows a rainbow to Hay—
books in the granary, the taverns, the castle,
Black Mountains calling.

      Some days are like this, forth and back,
      neither there nor here, all confusion, fatigue,
      and desultory verve. What else to do but brew
      passionfruit tea, sigh, pick up the book,
      turn to page ten.

WORDS AND PICTURES, SONG

Black and Red and Blue on White, 2022

after Mark Rothko

The near-blind great-grandmother paints the
sounds of her world, and stitches ragged
patches to old bed sheets that she's clothes-
pinned to the line strung from house to black
oak, heart-painted collages—true sounds,
true colors—frayed squares of her dead

husband's faded plaid flannel shirts, gauze-
thin dishrags, squirrels chortling in the
cottonwoods, cattle lowing in the lower
pasture, crimson crown feathers and juddery
yodels of high-in-the-sky sandhill cranes,

early-winter's frost-bearing wind, her
landlocked daughter's sea-blue eyes, puffs
of the red collie's undercoat and his whine at
the door at suppertime. Her sheet canvases

are Rothko-like, their music-colors part
lullaby, part gospel, and day after shrinking
day she paints and sews and listens to the
tints and shades of her long life, pausing
only to eat, to rest, to hang the next sheet.

Eudora Welty Writes a Story

Miss Welty scatters snippets of a story
on the ancient Aubusson (which has tales
of its own to tell), cut-apart paragraphs—
a doddering uncle, a bright and troubled girl,
a gossipy village, a small mystery, southern heat.
She kneels, straight pins from the sewing

basket gripped between her lips, rearranges
the snippets, pinning and re-pinning them,
looking for the whole.

On the curvy-legged table are stacks
of her black-and-white photographs—
a blind weaver; barefoot, skinny children;
women wielding scythes and shovels;
women resting on old porches; dark fields.
She hums, reads passages aloud, pencils in
changes and transitions, pauses to flip through
the photos, nodding, smiling.

She borrows a bit of France from the carpet,
just the color for the evening sun. When the story
is right, and when she's licked the last drop
of blood off her pricked fingers, she takes
the pinned-together sections to her desk, sips
a thimbleful of Maker's Mark, and gazes out
at the gardens—magnolias, of course, grandiflora,
and stately water oaks dripping with moss.

Beyond the gardens, beyond the mossy oaks,
live the strong women, the bright children,
the dark fields. She rolls a sheet of paper
into the typewriter and listens to their stories.

A Poem That Grew from a Mistranslation of Some
of the First Lines in Claribel Alegría's *Sorrow*

My grandmother told me a story about a kind of butterfly
that sings, one of the Gossamers. Only special children
and old women can hear their angelic voices.

They do not know where it comes from, but it is
the sweetest, airiest sound, rather like a baby's
murring in her sleep, perhaps a question for the angel

who watches over her and whispers about the way
to be in this world. They say a smiling sleeping baby
is dreaming about angels. I always knew I was one

of those children, a lovely flower whose name begins
with G—it might be Gardenia, I cannot remember.
You were from the sea; I did not know the seas,

but you lived in my pocket. My labyrinth is a circle,
yours all kelp and foam and angles, so I invented you
in the garden where I lived. Today is the night

of my sadness. You were my other me. When you went
away, I left my home to try to find you. Today is the day
of the Camellia, so I climb the hill. I say the word *love*.

What will it be like when we meet again? Everyone talks
to me about death. I do not want to live forever, and I, too,
die a little every day. I do not want to live with your ghost.

They say that death is solitary. I am not alone. My past
is with me, and if I fall asleep and dream that I am dead,
you will be there. My Gossamer wings are sure and luminous,
my petals fragrant. My angel's song is happiness. Give me
your song, your light, your warm hand.

Listening

The days shorten
and the snapdragons bluebells and coral bells
along the path
and the old collie dog sprawled on his back
belly bared to the silk tree's shade
      all seem to be listening
to Wesla Whitfield's "September in the Rain."
Wesla inhabits the song
      climbs inside
      throws open the windows
      rearranges the furniture
      makes it new
      makes it its own
      true sweet self.
Rainy September spills over the sleeping-porch rail
and Greensill plinks away on the jazz piano
      or perhaps
      the dog is listening
to the flowerbells tinkling
      or perhaps
      the blossoms are listening
to the dog's soft wheeze and tail swish
      or perhaps
      that sublime floating voice is listening
to dog to bluebells and coral bells to snapdragons
      quivering in the not-quite-a-breeze
and since this smoke-hazy day is my lucky day
      I am listening
      humming along
      to this late-June symphony
      all of us waiting for rain.

Art & Mathematics

In the museum she takes off running, jumps
into one of Thiebaud's slide-down-a-waterfall
streets, vertiginous & curvy, hops
into a fancy car teetering
on the crest of a hill, careens around
telephone poles & cars & UPS trucks,
down & around the steepest hills, makes a big
swoopy swerve through Marina Green, dodges
gamboling dogs, kite-flying kids,
tattooed nannies pushing strollers,
& heads straight on toward
white sails & whitecaps stippling the water,
bridges shining—one silver, one orange—
      helps herself to sweet-potato pie
      & a pinch of lemon-yellow 7-layer cake
      & listens to Mr. Tweed-Cap-Know-It-All
      intoning about Thiebaud's clever insertion of algebra
      & geometry into the streets, the cars, even the desserts—
      $x + y$, green (x), blue (y)—that building & that yield
      sign a perfect parallelogram, he says,
& she is in & out of the paintings, eating sweets,
feeling the salty, foggy air swish by as the fancy car lurches
uphill again past the chocolate factory, & she thinks
about the fat-bottomed bowls cupping a scoop
of vanilla &, oh, that hot fudge, waxy coating
on her tongue, whipped cream as white as isosceles sails
on the bay in fog-filtered Thiebaudesque light.

Defining Ourselves

In a picture-book Webster's, under
"unbelievable" or "harebrained idea,"
you might find circus elephants balancing
on tiny stools, their almond-small wet eyes
empty,
de-clawed bears riding tricycles, monkeys
banging on tambourines, and a horse
clattering up dozens of steps
to a wobbly platform and diving into
a not-so-deep pool, the relentless sun
an aloof observer.

Let's put a girl in a red spangly bathing suit
on the horse and watch them dive. And if one
of them lands wrong, breaks a leg or ruins
her eyes, let's train a new horse and praise
the gutsy girl for coming back for more.
Let's give them names like Lizzy and Lottie,
say, or Red Lips and Sonora. Let's watch the girl
on the platform casually paint her own lips,
turn a slow turn, sketch a blind wave, and climb
onto the horse, clutching his mane in her fists.

Let us admire the divers' beauty, their grace.
Let us feel the splash that shames
and defines us all.

Flames on Wheels

...the figure 5 / in gold / on a red / fire truck / moving tense...
—William Carlos Williams, "The Great Figure"

In the city
red and gold streak to orange
flames on wheels hurtling to danger disaster
heartbreak   banshee wail cutting the night
warped symphony.
Bold number 5 blurs to fire-brimmed waves
reek of sulfur   sizzle of plastic
melting. A corner of the world gone wrong.

Two blocks away
on Calle de Los Perros
ash steals through barred
screened windows.
A child whimpers.
The dogs twitch awake.

Watching the Sky

All at once he is no longer young / with his handful of flowers...
　　　　　　—W.S. Merwin, "Young Man Picking Flowers"

All at once he is no longer
and yet he will be always
in the beginning and in the forgetting
in the young man picking flowers
frangipani perhaps whose scent calls up
what's been forgotten but not forgotten
and in his dreams of wood thrushes
of swallows blackbirds
of morning sparrows
of the garden at dawn and the watching sky
he sees his grandmother watching the sky
and his mother always looking back wondering
and he wanders down the small roads
following the dog following the sounds
hymns for his father
bells and bleating dying sheep
the old voices and the new
wandering always in wonder
at the trees without names
at these green hills
these sun-hit fields
these dark mountains on these blessed days
at the vespers hush in the gloaming
at the imperfect that remains perfectly imperfect
at the unfinished that now is finished

Love's Latitudes

—The Rules of Painting with Oils (Rules to Follow or to Break)—

Be sure to use red, at least a dot, a dab, a smear of red,
        even if your red winds up palimpsested 7 layers deep.
Your subject should never be smack-dab
        in the center. Place it up a bit, to the right a bit
        (down a bit, to the left a bit can be unsettling,
        though that's not necessarily a bad thing).
As with planting trees or shrubs, do not paint even
        numbers of items, always 3 or 5 or 7 or 9.
Always paint the sides of the canvas.

Start with a yard-sale large painting, square,
        36" x 36", say, populated with another
        painter's dreams, perhaps unfinished with patches
        of bare canvas.
The one you choose might feature fuzzy-skinned monk seals
or foods—an avocado half, flesh browning; a cantaloupe slice;
        a saltine; a glass half full (or half empty)
        of what could be chocolate milk or zinfandel...
or garments—ripped-knee jeans and a red beret
        with dainty moth-holes...
or an open book with a broken spine, one legible word on the cover—
        "this."

Lay out your fine brushes, your palette knife. Open the tubes,
        inhale the incense of linseed oil, walnut oil, lavender oil,
        and begin.
Paint a rustic wooden table under a leaning backyard linden
        beneath a troubled evening sky (cerulean blue,
        pale rose blush, zinc white)
and on the table, avocado toast on a chipped china plate ringed
        with thimbleberries, 3 or 5 or 7 (cadmium red light),
and at the edge of the unmowed lawn, a patch of coral bells
        (titanium white), a hazy memory of an old campfire song,
        Oh, don't you wish that you might hear them ring?

Name your painting "Latitudes of Longing" or "Love's Apogee"—
    that moment, the brink, when love hovers, stops rising,
    and drips down the other side.

The coral bells *will* ring.
    Finally, beyond the tree you'll paint the shadow
    of a girl and a faint word (yellow ochre pale)—
    "this."

WHAT MATTERS

Ornithology

Birds I have never been   never known   never seen—
Flamingo   Spoonbill   Sad flycatcher
Bar-tailed godwit   Blue-footed booby

I—After Reading Wendell Berry's
"The first man who whistled thought he had a wren in his mouth…"

When I opened my mouth to sing,
a house wren flew out—feathers swirling,
chirping like crazy—and, trying again to find
my song, I watched the tiny bird circle the butterfly
bush that never grew a single butterfly, not even a moth,
and waited for the new strong alto voice I hoped would rise.

Birds that used to be—
Seychelles parakeet   Réunion sheldgoose
Laughing owl   Elephant bird
Great auk   Marianne white-eye

II—Flocking Together

There were no birds in my childhood. Unless you count Thanksgiving
turkeys. Or chickens on the farm in the cubbies in the coop—
sneeze-inducing straw motes, feather motes, dust motes. Airless stuffy
smells. Always the cranky hen (I called her Frieda) declining to give up
her treasure—squawking, pecking my fingers as I tried to ease the warm
egg from under her matronly pillowy self. Gentling the six or eight eggs
into my basket, I wondered which yolk would hold threads of red.
One of Frieda's? She was the chicken I wanted to be.

Birds that never were—
Great Plains penguin   Three-legged magpie
North Pole toucan   Percy Shelley's wert

III—Red-tailed Hawk Wakes the Morning

soars   screeches   two   insistent   syllables   claiming the air

dipping and gyring   higher   highest

keens   I am
        I am
                                I am
                                        I am

Birds I would never want to be—
Turkey buzzard   Pigeon   Woodpecker
Shrike   Rooster

IV—Black Phoebe and Crow

The day his father died, a black phoebe struck
   the glass, dropped into the ivy, staggered,
   shook feathers, flew up and away
The day her father died, a bird, same phoebe
   or phoebe's cousin
        window   ivy   stumbled and sagged   lay still
At twilight she planted it among the deer grass where Fritz and Alice
   and Flynn and Flora keep company
Today, crow sits on the fence wire behind his family at the birthday
   table on the beach

Birds I have been   or have known   or want to be—
Red-shouldered hawk   Ruby-throated hummingbird
Ameraucana chicken   Cattle egret   Crow
Sandhill crane

V—Long Away and Far Ago

When I was a bird
      when the world was young
            when the air was pure
                  before there was death
I did not know *blue* or *east* or *time*
I did know air and wind and sun/moon/stars
I knew earth and sky, rain and cold
I knew my birds and our songs
We knew danger
I knew water
I knew today

One Early-Summer Day, Looking Back

Lying on my cot on the deck, I scan my dwindling patch of sky.
It's shrunk over the years as the oaks and cedars and pines
have blotted out more and more blue. Still, there are plenty of stars
to follow, and planes and satellites criss-crossing. A hawk screeches
from across the creek. A few bats scurry-fly under the eaves and one
by one settle upside down.

The day quiets and shrivels to shadows and soft light.

After dinner—arugula and watermelon salad, balsamic-glazed grilled
chicken breasts, bread and wine—we hear the usual two deer curl up
on the Shasta daisy bed under the maple, an October Glory, her leaves
shimmery-green now, but she is already pulling back sugars and,
come October, will wear her glorious red coat.

Mid-afternoon, inside, ceiling fans try to move the air. Alice the old cat
creeps up the stairs with the sun, one at a time, stretches, and climbs
again, cat-napping her way up the thirteen steps, yowling when she runs
out of steps, out of sunlight. I think about where we'll plant her, near Fritz,
near Flynn, when she dies. It won't be long.

Noontime, the jays and crows—they are cousins—fluster and chase and
carry on their endless raucous conversations. Three gray squirrels strip
dead branches from the lindens, filling their mouths with bark, ends
sticking out every which way looking like handlebar mustaches
gone wild (nest materials, I assume), and they scramble and chatter
their way up into the branches of the tallest linden.

Midmorning, I tidy the tomato plants that are trying to escape their cages,
tie tendrils to wire, pinch off a few yellowing leaves, pull weeds
along the berry rows, check the few hard small nectarines for bird pecks.
This year I swear I'll get the fruit before the birds do.

I wake to the red-shouldered hawk's keening and watch as he gyres up
above the pines and swoops down, his early morning survey complete,
to perch atop the bar of the swing or on a fencepost or on a low branch
of a particular ponderosa. The hawk has been here every day for a week
or so. He will soon move on. It will be hot. It will be a good day.

Social Dissonance

March 26, 2020

Last night my daughter and I walked our dogs around
our neighborhoods together, one hundred fifty miles
apart, the dogs sniffing at bushes, vigilant—my daughter
beneath the Indian-maiden mountain, not far from

the aloof Pacific; I in the snowy-mountain foothills,
the Sierra Nevada, a few minutes from the wild
and scenic Yuba River, claimer of many lives each
rushing-water season—the four of us for this brief time

safe under the waxing crescent moon, under bright
Venus and Ursa Major, talking about children, about
fears, old and new, about the uncertainty of hope,
as if we were a mere social distance apart—

except we were not—not knowing when or whether
we might again be only two hearts' distance apart.

Life Plans

Luck is a tree branching to the roof / outside your window.
—Stanley Plumly, "Valentine"

Is it true that you make your own luck?
If you fail to believe, will you fail every time?

I will paint pictures of a cottage in the shade
of three lindens down a lane in the country
near a creek and pretend that I live there
with children and lilacs and long summer days.

I will swim in the pond and welcome the ducks,
make music, plant berries, raise chickens.
I will read through the night and get lost
in the woods, write letters and mail some of them.

Come winter, I'll hunker, build fires, bake bread,
work puzzles, knit sweaters and mittens.

The road will be long, journey's end a faint
shadow, but I'll set off tomorrow with hopes
for good luck and unsettled weather.

Breathing Lessons

Find your breath, the yoga teacher says, as if I've misplaced
it or tossed it into the recycle bin along with yogurt tubs
and yesterday's news.

Last night I dreamt again about the river, about rivers. I am
ever drawn to rivers, to their never sameness, their indifference,
their different way of breathing.

I woke to the breath of coffee and cardamom.

The two best things about my yesterday—

> the neighborhood fox and the old calico cat
> next to the berry fence staring one another down,
> close enough to smell each other's earthy breath,
> their standoff ending with a shrug, a nod, a turn-
> around, the fox blinking first
>
> and two Canada geese swooping in for a waveless
> landing in the pond in the pasture that belongs
> to a pair of ageless donkeys—

all of the above finding their own breath, taking in good
air, sending it out to mingle with Earth's aspirations.

Last night's new moon in hiding, the river of the Milky Way
pulled in all rising exhalations and rained them back—
indifferent blessings, another chance.

Fire Season

I'm thinking about air caught
in pockets—arrested, ensnared,
N and *O* gases jostling,
warm, brown, wet air in halfcup
of morning's dark roast.

Or haze in closed-up house,
smoky, a different brown.
Or in wild fires raging miles
away up forest canyons,
the air there red, hellish.

Hummingbird sips from red-petaled
blue-glass feeder, then perches
on potato rock on deck rail, then rises
to dip beak and drink, then perches,
then drinks in more cool blue and whirs
up and away, air and water warming,
thickening inside him
or her.

White hibiscus blossom, purple-hearted,
cradles smoky air. My lungs, too,
are browning,
air in my empty cup   gone,
air in that forest   beyond heat,
still angry, still red.

Last night from thinnest air,
an indifferent black sky shot stars,
hundreds of stars, heedless, random,
too cold for comfort.

Guten tag / Hwyl fawr

Until I was eight I believed in Santa Claus and the Tooth
Fairy, or maybe I was three. I don't much care for Hallowe'en.

I've brought home jars of dirt from St. Stephen's Green and
County Clare; sand from Provincetown; lava crumbs from
Kauai; a teaspoon of earth from a farm near Arlington, where
my mother played and drove the tractor. I have agates from
Wyoming, gorgeous blue sodalite from Montana (especially
gorgeous when it's wet, I've never been to Montana); and a
prairie agate and milkweed pods from Nebraska.

I wonder when we started having celebrations of life instead
of funerals (not that I think celebrations of life are a bad idea).
My grandmother had an album of dozens of photographs of
old people in their coffins. She knew who they all were. Now
none of us can identify any of them, except for blind Elmer,
his white cane laid diagonally across his chest. I didn't take a
photograph of my grandmother in her blue dress, in her blue-
satin-lined coffin. I have a shoebox filled with World War II
letters from my father to my mother. I haven't read them.

Once, riding the M streetcar from San Francisco State to my
afternoon job on Sansome Street, I fell asleep with my head
on a stranger's shoulder; he woke me at the Ferry Building
turnaround, and I had to walk back several blocks. I was late
to work. Another time as I was standing on a center island on
Market Street watching a motorcade bearing a waving Charles
de Gaulle pass by, I slipped off the curb and a man pulled me
to safety. Not the same stranger.

One winter, Uncle Ed tied a train of our sleds to his tractor
and pulled us up McGinnis's hill and we slid down, again and
again. Afterwards, we played Fox and Goose in the snow on
the lawn until it grew dark and we started running into each
other. When Uncle Alfred died in a car crash, I learned a new

word—"fatal." At the sandpits we watched as men pulled the body of a swimmer out of the water and laid him on a blanket. He was blue-blotchy, and I dreamed about him every night for weeks. My mother never learned to swim.

I have a hard time with directions; just tell me to turn right at the third stop sign, turn left at the 7-Eleven. I'm troubled by the growing squishiness of language—using "hone in," instead of "home in," for example. Or "enormity" instead of "enormousness." Let's reserve "enormity" for great wickedness, evildoings, depravity—such as slavery, cruelty to animals, separating immigrant children from their parents. Those crimes and sins deserve their own strong, undiluted words.

If I come back as a bird, I'd like to be a sandhill crane, though I'm not all that fond of flying or of cold. The Perseids are my favorite sky exhibit. There's something both beautiful and terrifying about rainbows. I want to write a poem or a story about a circus girl who runs away to join the Girl Scouts. There's not much sadness in March or April that a row of lilac bushes can't relieve.

I like the way the full moon rises, big and peachy, then settles into its usual size, its usual blue-whiteness. I like that "aloha" means "Goodbye" and "Hello."

The Way to Alone

Because there's been an alarming increase in pedestrian crashes, some of them fatal, for their own safety and the safety of others, the Heads-Down Tribe walkers, the phubbers, most of them ear-budded, have their own lane alongside Xi'an's largest shopping mall, quarantined from the rest of the world. The rest of us feel a kind of sadness as, unseeing, they stroll past one another and past the windows of the fancy shops—Manolo, Jimmy Choo; headless mannikins sporting Vera Wang, Chanel, Hermes, Prada, yada yada—ignoring the "Please don't look down for the rest of your life" messages painted on the lane, on their silent phubbing way to smartphone thumb, postural kyphosis, psychological disconnection, tunnel vision. On their way to alone.

Twenty years ago, we might have been the only white faces in that walled city. Aliens, we walked the streets, receiving curious nods and random smiles. A few times over our two days there, a woman or a girl approached our daughter and stroked her blonde hair. Outside the Kentucky Fried Chicken restaurant, a young woman, perhaps nineteen or twenty, wearing a shapeless brown cotton dress, eyes fixed on her shoes, hands folded at her waist, stood in public shame next to a hand-lettered board detailing her offense, large or small; of course, we couldn't read it. Flocks of pedestrians gave her a wide berth, gave her stern looks.

Today, under shopping malls and offices, freeways, schools, fields of corn and watermelon, still stand, have stood for millennia, stoic and strong, fixed eyes dust-shrouded—tribes of terra-cotta warriors, horses, scholars, farmers, kings, an occasional queen or noblewoman. Clay chariots at the ready, they wait for sight, for light, for breath.

What Matters

I want to know—
after this life—that is, in the afterlife
(if there is an afterlife)—
will there be pomegranates and kosher dills,
sourdough bread, frisky border collies
and six-toed sun-dozing cats,
willful children, novels, and *Swan Lakes*,
Willie Nelson and Kiri Te Kanawa streaming,
   or none of those,

and will there be an awareness of,
an occasional glimpse of, what and who
we were,
and will the wherefores of this life be explained
   or at least be able to be
   glimpsedly understood?

What matters now is the golding dawn rim of the mountain,
what matters now are the pink inside-out umbrella
   and the child-size pink rubber shoe on the rain-glazed street in Newark,
   and poems drifting out from First Baptist Peddie Memorial Church,
   and hard-boiled eggs and oranges in the Robert Treat Hotel,
what matters now are willful children, compliant children, children at play
   in the fields of our lives, and genial and gloomy commuters
   on the N Judah streetcar, especially those two or three pairs of eyes
   turned to real books (You remember books—those solid, hefty
   rectangles with worlds encased, bedecked with sticky notes or dog-eared
   pages and smelling of closets and bread).

She wants to know—
will there be summer afternoons,
will dawn always gild the rim of this mountain,
will there be fire?

Near Misses

The neighborhood owl (*Strigidae*) and the neighborhood mourning dove (*Columbidae*) never have a conversation, though they seem to share a language. The owl's song marks the moment when not-night turns night. The mourning dove's a daytime singer.

Robert Frost's farmer Warren said *Home is the place where, when you have to go there, they have to take you in*. If there's more truth to that than poetry, what are we to make of more than half a million unhoused persons in our country? Would each one prefer *unhoused person* or *homeless* or *residentially challenged* or none of the above?

The *I'll Clean Your Gutters* sign with tear-off phone numbers on the power pole on Nevada Street was replaced a month ago by *I'll Whack Your Weeds*. The gutter-cleaner/weed-whacker guy never returned my calls.

In San Francisco, my nine-months-pregnant friend Esther (this was years ago) hopped off the stopped-in-traffic bus and took off running down the sidewalk, her water breaking, sloshing her way five blocks to the hospital, her frantic husband Benny following, calling her name, and she delivered (Isn't that the perfect word?) *delivered* her perfect baby Melissa at the Geary Street Kaiser. Benny announced he should now be called Ben.

Two years ago we lost twenty-three ponderosas to the bark beetle (How many bark beetles does it take to take down a pine?). Not "lost," just dead or nearly dead, the trees too drought-weak to fill the beetle tunnels with pitch to save themselves. Next week, we'll lose another four or five.

Near miss is a misnomer—as in two cars careering toward each other and passing, front fenders inches apart—a miss, for sure. Near hit is what we mean—almost hit but didn't. They *did* miss! (That's one exclamation mark; I'm allowed only two a day, and the day is young.)

The locust tree on the bank near the swings fell in the middle of a March-night windstorm, its uprooted root ball as tall as a third-grader. Had it fallen some afternoon, there might have been a third-grader swinging—a hit or a near hit.

Just after dawn this morning (this not-night) two invisible planes made a nearly perfect contrail cross above the pines and cedars, their paths thousands of vertical feet apart, no danger of a near hit, but I took it as a promise anyway, a blessing for this day.

Washington County Tales That I Long to Hear Again but Cannot Because the Tellers' Voices Are Beyond

Tell me again about the boy who slipped his arms out of his homemade
casts and splashed into the coldish waters of Swift Fox Creek, laughing
at the minnows swarming and sluicing between his fingers, he loving
his skin-tingling life

and about that boy become a man who, off to court the pretty neighbor
farm girl one snowy evening, ran his car into the ditch and tromped
to the nearest farm and waited for the tractor to pull him out, and then
waited for the girl to come to the upstairs window in the middle
of the night and wave   and about that same girl who drove her mother
to town to buy fabric for a new dress and swept away the tire tracks
so the father wouldn't know

and about the man who walked miles to town each day trailed by the duck
that had a dog's name   and about Annie-on-the-Hill, pining for the tinker
who came to call every spring and fall with his spotted horse Fancy
and baskets of thread, spices, lavender sachets

and about the sweethearts kissing in the garden and the little girl
who saw them and thought they were dying   and about another girl
and her brothers playing with a shotgun in the barn and one of them, yes,
shot their beloved only sister (I remember her name but I won't say it)
—tell me, do you know what happened next

and about the farmer who lost a finger to the corn sheller and watched
stunned and bleeding as the banty rooster snatched his pinky and flapped
onto the cooptop   and about the smart, good-looking young man
who went off to the war and came back a different person, a quiet person,
and lived with his mother and tended the fields and the cattle until the day
he died—tell me, do you know if he ever had a love

and about the barn fire that long-ago November middle-of-the-night—
the burned calf and its mother, the team of horses, their panicked whinnies
sounding like a choir of screaming children ringing in your ears

and your dreams forever   and about the dapple gray that flew through
the flames and was never seen again

and about others who disappeared—the uncle who left a coffee cup
of coins on the kitchen table, walked out the door and down the lane
heading southwest   and about the man who lost his wife and his dog
and his crops and sat in his bedroom reading the Bible for days on end,
and one day hanged himself in the haymow

and about the great-grandmothers and maiden aunties who tucked
hankies into their sleeves and scolded the children and the misbehaving
men, but who also teased and baked bread and sometimes got to laughing,
and about the aliveness of those farm kitchens—the galvanized washtub,
the littlest ones bathing first and then the others, the water murking
and cooling, nightclothes warming atop the cookstove   and about
summer-evening fireflies and autumn's scratchy music of drying
cornstalks and cottonwood leaves.

Please—tell me again and tell me true. Tell me who I am or used to be
or might be one day, God willing and the creek don't rise, as the grannies
and the aunties used to say.

THE DOING AND
THE HAVING DONE

The Colors of Desire

A craving is wet isn't it
briny chartreuse
except when it's cobalt
wearing moonsheen

It's an inhalation
a clenching
a sort of fist

It's those few seconds
before you wake
when then and soon and now
possess you
your desires
mundane and strange
and you want all of it
yesterday
tomorrow
and this oval
cobalt moment

Coming Back

Why do they come back, and how
do they decide when to come back,
fluttering in dreams or alive

in the tottery walk of an old man
crossing the street against the red hand,
in the blur of a child spinning impossibly
fast on a creaky merry-go-round?

One gloomy winter's day, a boy with a false
name slithers through the side-porch door,
leaving a bedraggled black-and-white mutt
shivering under the arbor.

Why do we let them in, phantoms
of our unsettledness in this world
and our curiosity about before and after?
There's never any useful news

from the other side, only mixed-up
revisits—miseries and joys, wrong people
in wrong places, grandfathers the same
ages as their sons, their own grandparents.

These familiar strangers always float behind a wall
of watery glass, bubbled and crazed, figments
of memory's longing and confusions—
ashes and dust the potter mixes with water,

spins on the wheel, shapes and glazes
and tongs into the fire, making beautiful objects—
beautiful, yes, but breakable and cold and dead.

To Be Here

Let's banish the question
words altogether—
who, what, where, when, how,
why—
and erase the cartoonish
question mark.

Let's have a rolling-hills world—
with no chasms or Everests
of vitriol, tension, obsession,
with birdsong a more even register,
with howling winds ending in whispers
(there's never a question in the waves).
Let our talk be more song, more hum—
no need for raised voices,
no need for slings and arrows
in our even, fortunate world.

We could say *You're doing well,*
we could say *Tell me about that painting—*
those soft blues, the ripples, the shuttered house.
We could say *So happy you've arrived,*
however late.

If in the gray dawn we might wish for a way
to know the depths and heights our flesh is heir to,
let's tell ourselves
To be is enough.
To be here is enough.

Not the End of the World

The earth is not flat
No ends, no endings,
no true edges
on this bumpy sphere
No falling over the rim

into some borderless void
Walk toward the plains horizon
as it slides ever far away
Sail toward that dark stripe between sea
and sky and watch the stripe roll on before you

The lilac buds new florets while yesterday's
blooms turn brown
The turtle lays eggs
and trundles away from her young
The far side of summer

yellows in the dog-days air
The far reach of winter brings
crocus, daffodil, snowdrop anemone
When's the moment between
falcon's rise and fiery buckle

Where's the pause
between growth and death
Don't we begin to die
at the wet threshold of our lives
Wade your way toward love

forever after or toward the end
of what should have been love
and you'll only find yourself alone
back where you began

The Last

*"You will soon be crouching / Alone, with maybe some dim racial notion /
Of being the last, but none of how much / Your unnoticed going will mean"*

—James Dickey, "For the Last Wolverine"

The maple's leaftips are turning earlier this dry year, perhaps
the tree's last year (rather like the great-aunt who said
on her October birthday each year for the last ten or so
of her ninety-plus years that she wouldn't be with us
on her next birthday. No use to remind her: *That's what
you said last year and the year before that, dear Auntie).*

The maple is surely a hundred years old, about its limit
in this sad patchy lawn though it's been casually tended,
neglected just enough to stay beautifully shaggy, strong,
open-palmed.
In its heartwood does it know? Will it summon up
more maroon, less saffron for its final fall fling?

And what if it's wrong, has added maroon a year
or two too soon, tossed off its last samaras, thickened
its sap, too soon? Will the last samaras one day find
a patch of hospitable soil, shade, water and begin
again? Or will this be the last season
           promise
                glance
                        cross word
kiss?

How to say goodbye, so long, it's been good
to know you. Should old acquaintances, old aunties,
be forgot, will they truly be forgotten or remembered
in some unknowable way?
The boulder effaces,
        the glacier melts,
                shrinking to the last
                      cube,
to dead air.

Here and There

*There has been a meteor shower in the Chelyabinsk region of
Russia, 800 miles east of Moscow, with reports
speaking of hundreds of people injured.*
—BBC News, February 2013

Now that we've come through another storm—
wind-thrashed trees, frightened dogs cowering
behind sofas, hikers gone missing—we find
this afternoon hospitable, but in the Urals
the dawn sky falls, splashing into
an ice-choppy lake, and we hear the explosion,
feel the air and the ground vibrate even here—

ripples of fright like wind-borne invisible glass
shards or someone walking on our grandmothers'
graves. There, scavengers are gathering, collecting,
measuring, will soon be hawking the poor man's
black gold, and we will wait here for the next
explosion, trusting that Chicken Little and the Boy
Who Cried Wolf might be right, will be right,

eventually. Meanwhile along the creek
some bright greens are painting Douglas fir
fingertips, and in the thicket out back tiny buds
are tinged with the red of the berries to come,
come summer, though there may not be fruit,
or the fruit may be bug-spoiled,
or summer may not come.

The Dirt

You'll find the truth in the dirt
damp black honest dirt
Yes the truth and the lies and the silences
The orchid begins in green hush needing
no soil and giving up fragrance
for improbable   beauty

The baker crumbs yesterday's muffins
into tiered wedding cakes
The two-trunked cork oak fans wide
risks failure   holds

The boy's white hair turns brown turns
white in the sun
smells of summer   of wheat

The girl hopscotches to twelve turns
in the air   hops home

In your à la mode dreams you may die
then forget about death
forget the stars   and the green
and even the dirt

Hydrology

There are no virgin rivers,
not even underground ones,
not since before the serpent,
before the Red Delicious.

In the middle places,
hundreds of thousands of gallons
of cow shit and pig shit in barn-size
blenders spray across
hundreds of thousands of acres of pasture,
like some foul perversion of your backyard
sprinkler, and the besotted soil sends up
cloying grass/manure smells, sends down
poison into creeks, lakes, streams—dooming
fish, frogs, water skippers, lilies, hyacinths.

Miles away, a farmer has tried to espalier
his cleaner creek—digging; piling rocks,
logs, fence posts, old farm equipment;
shaping a serpentine beauty—but the creek
remembers where it belongs and gently pushes
aside his efforts. He's had better luck with his apple
trees—giraffe shapes, bears-on-hind-legs shapes,
hearts and tulip shapes—the Gravensteins smallish
but heavenly sweet.

We go to the abused waters anyway, pick up
trash, wade into the flow, arrange ourselves
over rocks, and soak up some of whatever
might be still alive there.

The Innocents

April 2011

Remember the innocents:
the lambs, goats, babies, virgins,
burned or stoned or starved
to bring an end to plagues,
pestilence, locust hordes,
to bring the rains, to stop the rains.
Their appeasing blood,
their charred and ruined flesh,
will save the rest of us,
will save the world.

They serve, willing or not,
though it's said that virgins
are honored to be chosen,
to be laid blindfolded,
white-gowned or naked,
across the smooth stone or
leaned against a wall or
some tree-of-life tree,
to welcome the sword or
the knife or rocks or fire.

Today, Tyvek-white-armored workers,
resolute, stoic, search for breaches
in the toxic dikes and stuff them
with concrete,
with sawdust,
with newspapers whose photos
and stories show and tell
of deluge, of ungodly
devastation.

Time and again, the boy in the story
slips his finger into the tiny crack in the dike,
feels the weight of the water wall,

feels the damp seep up his sleeve and spread,
so cold, across his chest and down his back.
He thinks of skating on that glassy lake,
of red and white tulips in the countryside,
of his picture in the newspaper,
of his mother holding
his skates and weeping.

To the Boy, To the Dog, To the Farmer

All that shimmers is not
greener on the other side.

Tell that to the boy standing
at the schoolhouse door, looking
over his shoulder at the lemony
half-halo topping the eastern hills.

To the whipped dog, yipping,
hightailing it
away.

To the farmer, tucking his bare feet
into cold Point Reyes sand,
his back to his faraway home,
salty winds all but blowing him over—
in those rolling whitecaps
he sees waves of grain
and dried cornstalks waiting
to be chopped down.

This morning's handful
of dew-glazed strawberries,
riddled with ants.

Warm pie on the sill, meringue
weeping pearls,
tart sun beneath.

Incandescence everywhere,
light-rimmed
promise and peril.

The Doing and the Having Done

The way to a poem
the getting there
between the journey
    and the destination
between the doing
    and the having done
laboring toward the having done
loving the having done
loving the doing   not so much

The having done
    pulling off tired boots
        and stepping into
        an August creek
    a perfect quilt with a planned mis-
        take
            three violet stitches spilling
            onto a golden floribunda
    a quiet, small but beautiful and wise novel
    a pared-down from hundreds of not-quite-right
            words to 143 just-right ones (best ones
            in best order)

The proof is always in the soufflé
though windage puts the maker/baker off
or the flit of swallowtails and honeybees
    in the butterfly bush
or the need for coffee for wine for water
or the call to clean the kitchen
    fold towels
    deadhead dahlias
to straighten
to rearrange
to dither
chary or *wary?*
ice-blue or *regret-blue?*

In the doing there's sweat
occasionally tears
rarely blood
toil   oh my yes
But now it's time to pick the last
blackberries
blend the dry ingredients
          (nice phrase
              dry ingredients
          pause to jot it down
          maybe make a poem with all kinds
              of dry
          a breezy August dog-days evening
          dusty windowsills
          feathers and rocks atop
              the bookshelves
          last year's oak leaves still
              hanging)
dot with butter and bake
eat the cobbler
lace-up the boots
thread the needle
write the poem

THE GIRL

Quercus Suber

The girl's secret self is tucked away in a hole in a cork oak
tree in the woods beyond the house. She likes the corky
sound of its real name, *Quercus suber*, loves the spongy
feel of its bark, its lemon-limey smell. She peels off chunks
to put in other hidey-holes—under her pillow or in a shoebox
buried deep in the closet.

It feels like a grandmother tree or a great-aunt tree,
and she wishes she could fit herself inside that cubby,
curl up with her treasures, imagines finding surprises there—
sticks of gum, coins, little soap people—like the treasures
Scout and Jem found in their special tree. She puts in her own
Ivory soap carvings of butterflies and birds and hearts,
a sap-sticky deodar cone, perfectly round pebbles, a lock
of her own straight brown hair held together with a newspaper
rubber band and tied with a scarlet birthday ribbon,
even snowballs in winter.

Next spring, the cubby's a mushy mess and she
cleans it out, starts over, tosses in words she likes—
perdido, cerulean, somersault, Afghanistan—
and hopeless hopes and dreams and wishes—
to be an only child with parents to sing her to sleep,
to read to her; the ends of stories she doesn't want to end;
ideas for stories she'll write one day, stories with pretty
words and bad words; and little meannesses—
sharp sticks to poke out some wicked person's eyes.
She imagines someone finding her tree, her trove,
her words and her stories.

As she walks back to the noisy house this April morning,
carrying a handful of fresh bark, she spies a red ribbon
fluttering from a nest in the deodar, just beyond her reach.

Paper Wings

The girl catches moths in her homemade net, takes a pinch of cotton
and dusts a smidge of powder off a papery wing, then watches
the brown creature fly in circles, one wing dipping, or waddle around

on its little moth feet. She studies their paisley wings, delicate
and intricate, like the lacy skeletons of last year's sweetgum leaves,
dried and bug-chewed. Maybe moths once *were* sweetgum leaves,

or vice versa, if reincarnation works with bugs and trees. The girl
thinks she was once a gazelle, once a Russian princess. The lunas,
though, are too beautiful to toy with—magenta-edged green wings

and fluttery tails, fuzzy purple antennae, and too big—
they would spill over her palms, and too fairy-like—
swimming around the porch light in a parade ring of June bugs

and lesser moths. In the afternoons, a few lunas cling to the shaded
barn walls, upside down and upside right. The girl draws close,
wondering if those wide-open eyes-on-wings see her, see anything.

One day, she captures a luna and puts it in the fridge until dark,
then lays it on the porch-swing seat and swings and waits as it comes
back to life, gives a moth version of a stretch-and-yawn, steps forth

like an airplane taxiing, and lifts off, gyring up to the birchtop-riding
moon. In her next life the girl wants to *be* a luna moth, surprising
some moth-come-back-as-child with her own fancy fairy

green-and-purpleness. If the child tampers with her wings,
that will be all right, and the girl will spiral up to the moon, rising
to what she will become after her brief, shimmery girl-moth life.

The First

When the baby felt
that first dry kiss
on her forehead she knew
she'd come into a place
of love
and confusion

The first girl who saw
a red-shouldered hawk wondered
if she'd met
an alien cousin
the girl's hair the color
of flame

The girl who heard
the hawk's keening
in the madrones across the creek
thought the world was coming
to an end and that she
was the first
to know

The girl who stepped
into the sea for the first time
tasted the briny air
smelled the rotting kelp
knew she'd been there before
knew she should turn away
before the waters claimed her
again
but she paused
feet sinking in sand
waves pulling like love

Reading by Snowlight

On full-moon nights she reads by snowlight
as winter girls might have done before the lightbulb,
before oil lamps, kerosene lamps, before candles—
those early girls reading stars and dreams. Words ring

more true in cold bluelight, away from woodstove
firelight, away from anger, from despair—
no kerosene film wafting words to brain via nose,
via eyes. On moonbright nights, few stars are brave

enough to show themselves. She reads about warm
places, dry places, arctic desolation, plucky children,
faithful dogs, impossible losses. You'd think she would
dream of, would long for, the tropics, sandy beaches

with seas stretching to the edge of the world—but no,
she waits for cold and colder, and then the burn sets in.

Zero in Kyiv

Zero degrees Fahrenheit in Kyiv today—
and yesterday and tomorrow and tomorrow.
The girl thinks that zero should mean nothing,
be just a pause, neither cold nor hot,
not one soul-chilling day
after short day
after dark day.

Afraid to go outside,
she fears her bones will freeze—
and then what?
She longs for the swelter of summer,
even the smelly air, the oppressive dank—
the imperfect perfection of August,

peridot at its center. Not the perfect gem,
not the luminous, deep-pool green—
she wouldn't know what to do with such purity.
She holds her small treasure
up to the weak winter light—
a cloudy, mottled stone—
and stares at its heart,

the peridot's own zero,
a speck of winter,
bone-white, frost-white,
and waits for green and white
to warm her rough red hands,
her rough red life.

Girl, Waking, Walking

Sand in her eyes every morning. The sandman, a scary
sprite, sprinkles it every middle of the dark. Some nights
she can feel the whispers of his wings and sand sifting

down as she drifts through sandy dreams, walking
through fields or on a summer lakeside beach
or down miles of dim city streets, some cold city

where she's never been—gray and strange and vacant.
A splash of cold water clears the grit and opens
her eyes to a tiny spider dangling from the beam

on its silky trapeze, the beam where last summer
two columns of ants, hundreds of ants, passed
each other, and where on another day an off-course

hummingbird perched, confused and fluttery,
before it could be coaxed toward an open
window festooned with a red bandanna.

But this morning it's only the spider, still spinning,
and the clear-eyed girl, still watching, still waiting.

Syzygy: The Full Long Nights Moon

Farmer yoked to plow to horse to straight furrows that
run from barn to drying-up creek Barefoot girl old
dog at her side leans against a leaning fence   The
three a kind of Earth drawn to this strange moon in dry
December air

This is the night the world might end
the night the world should end and the wobbly Earth shrink
from light to shade to darkest night evaporate
There'll be no pain no sorrow not a whimper just
momentary clarity then oblivion

Jupiter that
old bully pulls and everything begins to end
The farmer dead to the world cries out from his green
dream   The horse in his cheerless stall shuffles nickers
a low response

The girl smells wood smoke tastes honey The dog quivers
gives a silent cold howl lies at her feet and they
watch the Full Long Nights Moon turn fire red and the flames
flicker and die swallowing the night and soon all
the lights go out

SOME OTHERS

Whose Blue Heaven?

The sky is blue because we call it blue—
sun-scattered bits of dust and gases,
not the same blue as "Blue Moon" or "My
[or your] Blue Heaven," though of course
my blue/blues isn't/aren't anything like your
blue/blues and certainly not like Cousin Susie's.

Colorblind, "color vision deficient," she's never
seen blue, at least not my blue or yours. If you'd
asked her the color of her shirt or of that new
red Prius, she might've said, *Brown, I guess,*
not that her brown is my brown or yours.

Today, she lies on her Petaluma hospice bed facing
the wall, her thin winglike arm rising as if
on marionette strings, her knobby index finger
sketching endlessly on the white wall—
perhaps pictures of birds or of her beloved brother
or daughter or granddaughter or of her own heaven—
all blues or browns or some wondrous,
luminous color with no name.

A Bridge Not High Enough

She stands on the old bridge
a bridge too high not high enough
rust and gray wood
the falls upstream a sparkling
tumbling vertical mirror
of the tumbling
sparkling river
a tumble of sunsplashed granite
boulders climbing the banks.

She pauses then drops a silver bracelet
watches it swirl and catch in the rocks
its violet stones beckoning.
Slipsliding down the path
she wades into slimy pools at river's edge
reaches out to fetch the bracelet
careful not to step into the rushing cold
but the current carries it out and away
along with a small manzanita
roots and all.

The wader sees in the shallows
        gold flecks and glass shards
        flipflops and beer cans
        minnows
        water bugs
        plastic sixpack fish deathtraps.

She's up to her midthighs
pantlegs drenched
the river spraying her showering her
the sound sublime
emerald-green and sky-blue splashes crashes
and there's a faint eerie whistling
trickling from the falls

perhaps the song of the old Nisenan woman
who walked upstream one long ago
March cold-fast-river time and vanished.
Her song rings clear on moonless nights.
Perhaps the wader will come back
when next the moon is down and listen
for the wraithy violet and silver tune.

Supermoon Night

She chooses the supermoon night for her moonlit
walk, wants to step into that huge rising sphere
sending light across Tahoe's black water, calm
tonight, both she and the lake, obligatory stones

(nine of them, one for each reason) in her pockets—
coat, shirt, trousers—and one heavy, gray-and-white,
river-smooth stone in each hand. Though the sky
is moon-washed, she hopes to see the Aquariids,

and toys with this idea: If she counts more than
a dozen, she'll turn and go back...to where?...
for more...of what? She forgets the dying stars,
the moon, and wades into the lake, moves

resolutely deeper, not feeling the cold,
her determination fierce as she drifts down
and down, eyes open, the moon-drenched
waters so very beautiful, until long past

awareness of light or dark or why, she
settles on a branch and joins the others
in this spectral forest, some nearly as old
as the trees, along with animals from marmots

to wolves to deer and every one nearly whole.
The stories grow. It's said that in mid-summer
if you follow the wavery sun shafts, you can see
impossibly deep into those pure waters—

hair and needles, bark and fur, hooves and arms,
all suspended in ethereal light like floating
constellations, like the end and the beginning.

The Woman on C Street (or D Street)

The woman on C Street (or D Street)
—green stucco cottage, geraniums—
fears her mind has gone missing, can't

remember where or when she lost it,
hopes she's merely misplaced it like her
sunglasses (the top of her head? the fridge?)

or car keys or celery seed and dill weed absent
from their alphabetical slots. However,
she does remember *hippodrome, hippocampus,*
hippopotamus, is good at Word Jumble,

pretty good at Sudoku, remembers to make school
lunches for dogs, remembers to take kids
to the vet (or would if the kids were still here),

is her own oldest best friend, talks to herself
(no problem with that, gets only right answers),
has moments—hours!—of clarity. Her hit-and-miss

friend (on vacation?) turns up now and again like
a lost mitten after its orphaned mate has been tossed.
On this balmy spring evening she sits on the stoop,
dog leashes limp across her lap, pondering, worrying—

thinks about trying a trade, throw away something
she loves, something dear—the old clock with the girl
in the swing (the girl looks just like her Lucy), will

leave it at the curb with a free sign, or, maybe,
she'll give up an eye or the use of an arm (not sure how
she would do this), a sacrifice, a deal with the god

she's never believed in (maybe it's not too late to believe).
Tomorrow, perhaps, she'll find all that's gone

missing, a surprise on her doorstep—her best friend;
a May basket spilling over with sweets; an infant

swaddled in a beach towel, pink chubby arms flailing.
Rising, the woman on C Street (or D Street) pats the night
air and goes into the house, dog leashes trailing.

The Places Between

The two lived for years in a house with no walls
in a valley between sea and mountain. If
they climbed the mountain, not a very tall one,
they could see the sea, though they rarely
made the effort, just endured those decades
between drifts of salt air and mountaintop clouds,
between light and dark, mostly in shade,
between love and not-love,
among owls and the occasional gull, a lone
brown bear, hawks and wild turkeys, mouse-tailed
bats hanging and swooping.

There were random dogs, near-feral cats.
There was never a child.
Recluses, soulmates of a sort
(though they'd foresworn the idea of soul),
they nodded to their few neighbors,
likewise hermitic, on rare trips to the village
around the dark mountain.

Days, weeks passed without words, as they watched
the clouds and breathed dank briny air.
They made austere art from bark, wildflowers,
bird and animal teeth and bones, red clay—
delicate pieces only the two of them would ever see—
made it, moved it from inside to outside,
then buried it along with the others.

In Sheep's Clothing

She's forgotten how to knit—all those booties, sweaters, hats,
her old hands still soft and wrinkle-free, lanolin-fed…

> The dog on the hearth used to know sheep—how they smell,
> how they think (puny brains though they have), what it means
> when their eyes, all fifty or a hundred pairs of them, go glossy
> at the same time…

and how to bake an apple pie—flaky crust, lard and flour and salt,
hand-picked apples, scrubbed not peeled, a little sugar, a little cinnamon,

> how to gather them—the stare-down, the yips
> and nips, show them who's boss, watch them quiver,
> the sheep thinking Wolf!

but she's not forgotten pearls of sunlight floating on the creek,
she's not forgotten the babies—the small dents pulsing on the tops of
their heads, their sweet-smelling necks, their warm bodies covered
with down—as soft and as helpless as lambs…

> Her fingers remember, twitch, and the dog stirs, stretches long,
> paws tufts of wool from his teeth, hears from the far distance
> a chorus of bleats and the man's faint praise, *That'll do…*

and new voices rise as the wolves circle, the dog unable to save them.

Autumn Preserves

The near-blind great-grandmother makes autumn
jam in the woods, her pestle and mortar a madrone
burl and a water-sculpted, granite-boulder bowl.

Tweets and creaks and swishes a soft music
around her, she grinds hazelnuts, sugar maple
samaras, foraged mystery seeds, and dried
blackberries pulled from October
brambles that line the paths between

her cottage and the forest center's dark
heart. She sings to the bees, filches a pinch
of honeycomb, stirs it in, scoops the mishmash
into the old blue milk bowl and carries it
to the cast iron kettle, the Copper-Clad cookstove,
the mason jars, and hums as she stirs and funnels.

In the rising steam, December appears—
the children, the grands and the great-grands,
cozy in her parlor. She'll bake acorn-meal
scones, steep chamomile tea, sniff Indian-
summer heat rising, and she'll break open
a scone, spread jam, and take bittersweet
autumn into her mouth.

The Other Heaven

On nights with little moon or none,
the near-blind great-grandmother settles
in her chair in the middle of the orchard,
bare branches or new leaves or hard-green
or just-right or too-late pears
around her, depending,

and listens to the music of the spheres. She makes
a circle, a kind of moon, with thumbs and pointers
touching, and looks up through it to where the sisters
or the queen or the swan might be and waits
for the tunes to begin—whistling or humming
or bluesy harmonica or plaintive fiddle, sometimes
(she smiles at this) a harp,

and all of it, lullaby or symphony, faint and strange.
Oftentimes, she stirs to find the night sky gone
and rises to the crackle of the sun waking up the pears.

The Speed of Firelight

When the girl asks, "When is Papa
coming home?" they're sitting in the glider,
watching the lively night—the orangey,
smoke-shrouded crescent moon, the lightning
bolts that threaten to set more Jeffreys
and aspens and lodgepoles ablaze. No deer
tonight, no foxes, no owl's lonesome call. Thunder
rolls around them, quieting even the crickets.
The girl counts elephants after each jaggedy flash.
She is not afraid. The woman pulls her closer
and begins in her wistful, storytelling voice—
"Maybe some blue-moon time. Or
maybe when the cows come home, swinging
their ropy tails behind them, or
maybe on the Twelfth of Never, or
maybe when Methuselah celebrates
his nine hundred seventieth birthday—
no cake, no candles for that old man. No, I'm
guessing your papa will show up some indigo night—
no fires, no lightning, just roll in at the speed
of firelight." The girl tastes smoke, rubs her eyes.
"Methuselah," she says, and counts more elephants.
She asks again, "When is Papa coming home?" The woman
sighs and says, "Oh, not tonight, Missy. Call the dogs in,
and let's have strawberries and a nice bath."

Jam Session

I

Every other Tuesday, 6 or 8 or 12 of them—toting ukuleles,
harmonicas, guitars, fiddles, maracas, and one musical saw—
climb the steep stairs to the Odd Fellows Hall above the gallery
next door to the not-quite-falling-down Gold Rush-era hotel,
which for years has sheltered mostly transients; occasional tourists
who walk its creaky-floor halls and sleep between questionable
sheets, hoping to hear or get a glimpse of the resident ghost
(said to be a murder victim in some 1850s mining-claim dispute);
and one (unless you count the ghost) longtime resident, part-time
recluse, who lives in Room 64 on the otherwise unoccupied
leaky-roof third floor and has filled her room with books
and cowboy hats and cacti, who orders takeout from the diner
across the street and cocktails from the downstairs bar and tells
anyone who'll listen that she often hears the ghost, has seen him,
watery and bluish, and some months ago more than saw him—
had a strange conversation, more mind-to-mind than actual.
The highlights of her days are checking out the tourists (who
sometimes spot her slipping around a corner and think she might
be the ghost), listening to the Tuesday music floating down
the street and up to her room, and tracking the ghost.
She calls him Martin.

II

In the early morning hours as the river keeper patrols her stretch
of the South Yuba, she might encounter bears, coyotes, or, once
in a while, people—goldpanners, early-morning hikers, down-
and-outers. She carries pepper spray and bear spray, fills
her trash bag with disgusting debris (occasionally a sock or shoe,
soggy diapers, a waterlogged copy of *On the Road*, a newish
red sunhat that she washed and wears). Her best find, the only
other thing she's kept, is the foreign rock she found last summer
among the poison oak and kitkitdizze (aka mountain misery,
aka bearclover). The rock is rough and bumpy, wet in the morning
dew; otherwise, she wouldn't have seen its incognito blueness.

Lapis lazuli, she guesses, lazurite and pyrite—it looks and feels like dark and light at once. It's against the rules to take home rocks or plants or artifacts. When she finds the rare obsidian arrowhead, she buries it beneath a sprawling manzanita or tucks it deep into the shade under a granite boulder. The back of her shirt reads *Leave Only Pawprints*. On occasional Tuesdays, the river keeper climbs the stairs and plays the flute. She always wears the red sunhat.

Time to Murder and Create

In the beginning there was no time—
gravity yes
but no left right up down
here or there
no grammar except the noun—
night day earth sea
salt heat critters people
but no Tuesday
no August.
When the verbs arrived
in some cosmic hiccup
they were "to be" verbs
present tense—
the dark is
the woman is
and then another hiccup
spewed forth the action verbs
simple ones at first—
eat run mate—
which quickly led
to need to desire to wish away
to make and
—no surprise—
to the making of art and poems
and tools and guns
and to art and poems
that celebrate the tool and the gun
but not to enough time
or proper nouns
or transitive verbs
to measure the distance
from then to when
to find the beginning
to settle the gathering dark.

WHAT HAPPENS

The First Day, King James Version, Revised

[on] the first day   god created the preposition   imagine
          the world   [without] them   there wouldn't be a world
                king james wouldn't have been   we wouldn't be
the world a stale and static flat   nothingness
          no beauty   no bodhi   only formless dark void

squirrel and hollow log would wait   still and puzzled
          squirrel   frozen   the log squirrel's *raison*
               [d]'être
no [under] it   no [over] it   [around] it   [through] it
          [near] it   [above] [inside] [outside] [beyond] it
that skittery brush-tail rodent would sit alone   be
          bored   attenuate   evaporate

day 2   the language [of] shakespeare
          who [without] the preposition wouldn't have been
               says
                    he created   light and dark
                         the day   the night

day 3   the firmament   heaven   the sky

day 4   dry land   the earth   the seas   the grasses   fruit trees

day 5   sun   greater light moon   lesser light   the stars

day 6   water creatures   whales all swimming things
          winged creatures   egrets all flying things

day 7   earth creatures   beasts   cattle
          creeping things   bugs
          man [in] his image
               grains   seeds   herbs
          nourishment [for] every sky   sea   land   dweller

day 8   the perfect number   an angel number   harmony
          the luckiest number
the language [of] shakespeare
          says
                god rested
          contemplating his greatest creation
                the humble   the hardworking   preposition

     making kansas possible   tasmania   the maple   the banyan
     the pomegranate   the raspberry   kale
     alstroemeria   cassiopeia   the moon's dark
     side   iceland   ice   the nile   the wallaby   the killer
          whale   the newt
                               the sandhill crane
     and   finally   woman   ribs and breasts   fibula and tibia
          heart

and god said that it was all good
          really good

and on the ninth day God created upper case—
          and punctuation!!!!

Mnemonics, or Useful Useless Information

George Eddie Otto Grace rode a pig home yesterday.
A rat in the house might eat the ice cream
       (a half-gallon of ice cream
       isn't a half-gallon,
       isn't real cream).

3 tsp = 1 T, 4 T = 1/4 cup or thereabouts,
and before the black-and-white of the X-ray
Ezekiel knew this: the thigh bone's
connected to the knee bone.

"2 bees or not 2 bees" has something
to do with whether
it's shirtsleeve weather
or time for earmuffs and fat mittens,
and red sky at morning means trouble.

It's 5,280 regular steps to the library
(or 1,760 really long steps).

She's never known a George an Eddie
an Otto or a Grace or seen a purple cow
though many a 3 a.m.-time she ponders
       the geography of arithmetic in lieu
       of counting sheep or ships
and gives herself word problems
and considers some of the problems with words:
       E.g., if the train leaves the
       Red Cloud station at 3 p.m. CDT, will it
       clatter in to the Oakland depot at 2 freckles
       past a hair, PDT?
       E.g., gnus and gnomes, knees and knives,
       pneumonia, pfeffernüsse,
       ravel/unravel, flammable/inflammable,
       through, tough, cough
       and the several other -o-u-g-h's

and wonders whether Jimmy and K-K-K Katy,
beautiful Katy, ever got together.

And when the m-m-m-moon
        (blue or strawberry or hunter's or wolf
        or sturgeon or gibbous waning or eyelash)
shines over the cowshed,
she imagines herself in middle-of-nowhere
Red Cloud, ready to board the eastbound train.

Rending Flesh

with apologies to Robert Frost

Something there is that doesn't love a gardener,
that sends out thorns and prickles, barbs and briars,
spines, stickers, needles, nettles, brambles, burrs.

Thorny shrubs and vines, Mother Nature's bad jokes,
lure us with lacy blossoms and towering, beyond-
our-reach clusters of blackberries, smelling of sundust,
wet sapphires filled with the fullness of summertime
and vitamins enough to ward off disease.

Don't we know these creatures well? Vegetative
porcupines, hedgehogs. Feisty, sneaky, mean. Lying
in wait.
Haven't we read about them all? Edward Bear's gorse bush,
Br'er Rabbit's briar patch. And lovely princess Briar Rose's
charming prince machete-ing his way through acres
of brambles. No doubt some blackhearted
barbed vines found their way through
the chinks in his shiny armor, and his princely
blood dripped on her chaste linen gown as
he kissed her berry-sweet lips.

In my backyard, shooting up here, there,
and everywhere are hawthorn, wild rose, blackberry;
it's like a prison yard zigzaggy with razor wire—
but I am trying to get in, not out.

In autumn, the hawthorn, *Crataegus*, weed tree,
makes berries to make drunkards of the birds.
Its ugly-duckling winter skeleton, all pointy
teeth and dried-up berries, turns
swanlike in the spring, white petticoat blossoms
hiding the barbs.

And there's a *Rubus*, rambling rose.
The deer, their lips and hides impervious,
pucker up and nip the blossoms,
but *Rubus*'s thorns pierce my jeans and
stab through the seams of my heavy gloves.

The most seductive thorny one? Another *Rubus*,
blackberry—tangled, braided, beckoning. My reward?
Thorn-raked limbs, blood and sweat and purple juice
mingling, running up my arms. Bumpy, fuzzy morsels
tasting of the sweetness of a summer dawn.

Perhaps it's Nature's way of balancing—
she gives the homely girl an angelic soprano voice,
a voice her off-pitch orchid-face sister can only yearn for.
When everyone sits around the fire on a late summer
evening and hears those crystalline notes,
that blackberries-in-the-sun voice,
Orchid thinks she might change
places with *Crataegus* or *Rubus*, even knowing she'd hate
herself come morning, come winter.

Sitting on the deck this August eve, a berry-colored sky
spread wide above the pinetops, I eat cobbler,
warm with cream in Grandma's bowl, and I cannot
help but lick my lips and say:
Good brambles make good berries.

Chicksimmons

If chickens were fruit they might be persimmons,
Hachiyas—those make-your-lips-pucker,
weather-predicting, seed-harboring,
not-exactly-beautiful-but-prettily-autumn-leaf-colored
squatty orbs...
      or, if vegetables, maybe prickly pear
      or Brussels sprouts...
      or, if people, spinster-teacher aunts
      who pile books on the bed and drink gin.

Chickens seem a serious mistake—
      their mishmash parts,
      their cold, haughty stares,
      their jerky strutting about
      on gnarly, witchy-fingered feet,
yet aren't they a kind of perfection—
      wattles and spurs, piercing marbly eyes,
      spiky Elvis pompadour combs—
comfortable in their goose-pimply skins
and oily feathers.

Even the dead one we met in the restaurant
in Linxia, China—its uncooked chopped-off head
atop the boiled rest of it on the table,
its dead eyes gawking at the skinned headless goat
hanging on the side wall, its black cloven hooves
looking like dancing shoes.
I have no idea what
to make of the goat's carcass
or where its head wound up.

(Something about *The Godfather*'s horse's-head-on-pillow
scene is trying to get a foot in this swinging door,
but I won't let it.
Who, after all, is in charge of this woolgathering?)
That floppy head seemed to nod, beady, persimmon-gold
eyes glaring at us, daring us, putting us in our places,
and, I swear, those dangling hooves
clicked heels.

Prairie Prom

What if some prairie chickens and sandhill cranes and maybe
a whooper or two threw a party when no one was looking,
not even the photographers in camouflage hunkered down
in their branch-roofed blinds with their long lenses, their
granola bars and thermos bottles. And what if the birds invited
some spoonbills and ibises, though the dance field might be
a bit frosty for those warm bloods. Picture conga line, bunny
hop: cranes preening and prancing, stocky chickens chortling,
scurrying about, stamping their feet, weaving in and out
through dozens of twiggy legs.

Prairie Doo-wop and Prairie Motown, rock 'n' roll, the twist.
Yodels and whoops. Eyes locking, eyes glancing away. Shaking
and clacking their pointy beaks, their curly beaks, their flat
beaks. A few shy ones huddling on the sidelines: wings tucked,
watching, longing. Can't you just see the slow dances, The
Penguins crooning: "Earth angel, earth angel, will you be mi...
ine, my darling dear..." Dancers' breath cloudlets. Wings lifting
and drifting, wingtips touching. Red, white, and gray feathers
swirling in the downy moonlight.

What Happens When the Tornado Swoops Up the Kitchen, the Library

sea salt and cinnamon, brown sugar and basil
pepper Tess's white gown as she slips the letter
under the door of the good man she'll marry—
the letter, of course, flies into the pea-green-boat soup—
garlic and onions, whipped, stirred, folded, sifted—
raw milkmaid, raw milk, curds
and waffles

Angel Clare brings devil's food pasta
to Miss Havisham who's watching Laura
and Ma and Pip pour maple syrup onto fresh snow,
and it bubbles away on the old cookstove
that hangs sideways, tree-captured and tended
by the red-faced girl feeding its maw with cabbages,
chairlegs, whatever, the corncobs having gone
missing

Gregor, growing weaker hour by hour, huddles
next to the toaster, his sister feeding him fresh dill,
Vidalia onions, wild salmon, white wine, and peas
porridge cold nine days old

but there's such peace on the simmering river,
such turmoil boiling inside the boy—
the audacity of Jim's wanting to steal...steal!
the cast iron skillet filled with rice pudding
and even his own wife and children, Huck's aiding
and abetting surely dooming him
to a hard boil, baked and broiled, chilled
and frozen

Peter Rabbit eats Poky's strawberries, a teakettle full,
and Little Red Hen shakes out her feta-dusted
feathers, lays a speckled shirred egg

and struts over dale and hill, sniffing vanilla breeze,
dodging turnips and blueberries
and doling out French toast and carrots
as the dish runs away with rosemary,
Olive Oyl, the dastard, the dupe,
the lovers, the changeling child,
the sly
and the lost,
the king
and the dunce,
the runcible spoon

Just Because I Can

sonnet, shake my life up.
chapter & then the last, write a 13-line upside-down
pluck a novel from the wobbly stack, read the first
my bed un-feng-shui-ish, crossways under the beams,

peels & all, drink cabernet with farm-raised salmon, turn
for ladders, buy a sack of Fujis, non-organic, eat a couple,
at city hall, borrow a stray black cat & go looking
in the left lane, park in a red zone, use the men's room

my fever, starve my cold azaleas, drive to town
prepositions, take vitamins with grapefruit juice, feed
of her long since at rest), end sentences with
about my mother's back, her weary back & the rest

Today I'll step on every crack (no worries

I Can't Even

The middle marmot
       there were three
                     twitching
in the median
           I-80

Yevgeny Yevtushenko
—or someone else—said
       poetess is the word for a poet's wife
His wives were
           Bella A
           Galina S-L
           Jan B
           Maria N
One of his poems begins
       No people are uninteresting...
                     I can't

The cotton reunion loomed
       new dog
       threat of rain
       difficult cousin
The jostle of that weekend
was exhausting
       mud
       chores
       unexpected
           nectarines
       mama bear and three cubs climbing
           down the crooked pine
                I can't

The madrone
       sleek maroon bark
       Arbutus menziesii
       decides
       it's time
              I can't even

The new planet named for an unknown poet
           disappeared

THIS DAY AGAIN

The Same But Different

So many ways to live twice or more than twice,
not all of them pleasant or worth repeating, but
unavoidable.

Humdrumnesses. Mundanities.

The laundry—
the same socks, the same darks and lights,
agitating, spinning.

The cleaning—
vacuum tracks criss-crossing
the same carpet, some other carpets.

The green-thumb attempts—
the same toothpicked
avocado pit in murky-water jam jar on the sill,
destined to reach only the ceiling—
Jack's beanstalk, no giant, no boy.

Et cetera,
but, oh, the beauties, the blessings—
The dawn, the twilight, the middle-
of-the-night cool wash of air
through the window.

The words and pictures—
picture books, soft splash of colors,
with the children, always the same,
always different, on the same lap,
wriggles and silences
and milky, grassy-smell hair.

Yet always, always—
the same and different questions,
the same and different forks in the road.
Any other way to do this?
Not really, only to hope for the great
good luck to live this day, this way again,
this same way, some different way.

July Mornings, Watching Bluebirds, Listening

Morning after morning, in the dawn's wan light,
two western bluebirds flash blue and orange
among the tallest black oaks, the Douglas firs,
the deodars, the ponderosas, their chitterings
bright sparks against the green.

They sound young and frisky, boyish,
sometimes harmonizing in sublime,
ethereal song, sometimes squabbling.
I decide they are brothers.

And then they're gone, each, I imagine,
taking his own path, adventuring—
one flying into the wind,
fierce wing-stopping stasis,
the other coasting in balmy currents
of least resistance, hoping they'll find
one another once again bird years later,
in October, say, back in my trees,
singing to me their travelers' tales
of other dawns and other trees (pinyon pines
and aspens), flights with cousins, danger tales,
pirate tales, country bird and city bird tales—
their autumn song in lower register,
their feathers rough, the oaks and conifers
dry and dusty, the maple fiery,
the dawn light weak and watery.

My folly—
to think they'll even notice me,
to even think I own these trees.

August, the Wee Hours

Too hot to sleep too restless to sit too tired
to read, I head for the door and collie dog
springs to life. Sliver moon waning perches
on a ponderosa across Deer Creek

and the low-down stars in milky wash do
their summer thing. The air goosebumps my skin
and I'm happy, grateful to be here, grateful
for night sky and sweet-smelling breeze.

Neighbors' windows are open, sounds drifting out,
Law & Order percussing, TV preacher exhorting—
The devil's amongst us, send money.
Now, music rides out on the scent

of a spice bush, violin—arpeggios, trills. Three
quiet dark houses, then a powerful snore
and a woman's voice—*Hey, coffee's ready.*
I almost call out—*Make mine iced decaf...please.*

We sit on the curb that holds yesterday's heat
and listen and listen and breathe, watch free-falling
Perseids and hunters and sisters and the moon
inching from pine to cedar. Red light

on the mountain. Sprinklers hum on, dog woofs
and I laugh. Time-challenged rooster
cock-a-doodle-doos. This night's not made
for sleeping. We stroll past a house that's lit up

like Christmas. On the lawn, bears and flamingos.
Silhouette He behind window shade asks—
Why did he leave her and where did he go?
Silhouette She asks—*Where's the remote?*

Tabby cat wades through the grass, collie dog
follows, tail swinging. I sigh and say—
Let's go round once more, hear what's on TV now.

Besides, I want answers—
Why did he leave her and where did he go?

Harvest Salad

I'm taking in the late afternoon
Indian-summer air,
a nice bronze weight to it
and autumn dust on my tongue,
turning in circles, despairing
of how to begin to address
this fine fall mess.
Green tomatoes hang
like so many
Christmas
bulbs,
run-amuck berry vines tangle
with dried sunflower stalks,
their browning, drooping
flower faces
turned to the earth,
and everything's powdered with light
the color those same blossoms recently
gave up.
I pick three not-quite-ripe
black-cherry tomatoes
and a handful of autumn-gold raspberries,
sit in the dirt and savor
these sour-sweet fall garden gifts
as if I might salt away gold to spend
some dreary January day.

Sky Writing

I will write my letter to the world and to my children
with a Chinese brush on newsprint with lime-flavored
soda water so I can think and drink and write
everything I know and don't know. I'll begin

in some foreign language I do not know or used to know
or want to know—Cyrillic script, perhaps, and switch
to Old Norse, Morse code dashes and dots, pig Latin
and old Latin—*veni, vidi, vici . . . Omnia Gallia
in tres partes divisa est.* It will take years.

When the water dries and the sheets are wrinkled
but clean and inscrutable, at low tide I'll abandon
brush and paper and drag my umbrella, ferruling
my way across the sand from when to tomorrow,
and then I will etch hectares of drought-dry earth

with a lilac branch to infuse the words
with color and nectar—necessary grit and sugar—
or simply push my finger through red-dirt dust
on old bureaus and pollen dust on window
sills, and finally trace Inuit words for *snow*

in the snow. When I finally stop writing in March
or November, I'll listen for my words in the soaring
language of cranes as they fly north or south—
amo, amas, amat, amamus, amatis, amant.

Once Before a Time

I wish I could remember who
I was 2, 3, or 4 lives ago. If we keep
getting better, as some say we do,
my next me will be taller, wiser,
braver, stronger, have better hair.
What did I learn

living in those other selves: where
did I live, whom did I love, hate,
fear, betray? Who may have loved
me? What explains my fear of, my
fascination with heights, spiders,
deep water?

Were my now children
part of my then lives? Is that what
déjà vu is all about? A place resonates—
air, light, smells and sounds—
because one of me was there once
upon a time.

One August on my birthday, strolling
through the courtyard of a Buddhist temple
in Linxia, China, we came upon old lilac
bushes—that spring-blooming, heavenly
fragranced flower is my favorite—but these
were gray-leafed,

scraggly, with skimpy, scentless pale blooms
(though somehow I could smell my own
front-yard lilacs). Everything loomed familiar,
even though China had shown me the meaning
of *Stranger in a Strange Land*. And I knew
that when I turned

the corner I'd see a slender, ageless white-robed
monk sitting on a bench, reading. Yes, he was there—
white robe, old books, more lilacs, lush, pretty
ones, bookending the bench. He did not look
at me. I wonder where I'll go and who or what
I'll be next time around.

When the Seas Were Prayers

Long away and far ago when trees were churches
and seas were prayers and wrens could talk,
you could look to the skyline and hear song—
mournful, beautiful song; children's-choir, earnest-
almost-tuneful-voices song. You could listen
to the winds and see and almost touch the rest
of your long life in swirling plum blossoms, and turn
each corner knowing that a sweet surprise awaits—

the child you were, the children you will have, even love
itself walking toward you in the blue-fog morning.
Although low clouds and the cards may tell you
otherwise, the wrens will let you know that all will be
well, and that the tree churches and the sea prayers
and the song blossoms will fill your life, however long.

Swimming Through the Dark

for Gene

The night grows dark but I'm not far from home
for where is home but here with him—
the lively, lovely children grown and gone.

In light I move from then to now with hope,
my days edged mauve and blue from eve to dawn.
On darkest nights I wander far from home

to swim in colors, rivers wild and calm—
at one with prairie, mountains, rocks, and trees,
the lively girl and boys not truly gone,

just miles away and swimming on their own,
their lives their own yet mine to visit and to love.
When home seems dark but I am far from night, alone,

my only light is dimmest other homes,
with wind and silence, rain-drenched curtains flapping,
and other girls and boys long grown and gone,

one swimming for the farthest shore from home
to join some others, wait with them...or not.
And now, still far from night in our light home,
I watch the mirrored boys and girl swim on and on.

At the End of the Day

Because I could not stop for air, I learned
that someone there is that doesn't love birdsong.
       Even though I live in this pretty how town,
       there's a fire somewhere else, not far from here,
       or will be, and even though on the porch railing
       there's sun tea brewing as gold as the runaway
       St. John's wort that's strangled the wild clematis,
I know that articulated buses in Seattle are still taking
the corners like ambling geriatric caterpillars,
       and the boy at the inn in Taxco is still sweeping
       the dirt and watching the revolving flirty young girls,
       and the green piñata spills broccolini, sugar peas,
       and organic grapes on the baby's tears,
       and the two-trunked oak threatens to split,
       to send its wider leg crashing into the copse
       of native dogwood, and day after day
       the water's edge warns and invites.
When the robot neurologist via video asks the patient
to raise his arms, his right leg, his left leg,
       the patient cannot,
       and I picture Lewy bodies as other planets,
       other stars that died dark years ago.
At the end of the day I go to sleep, except when I don't,
       and last night star jasmine and linden blossoms
       sweetened the air as one airplane, red lights pulsing,
       and one satellite sailed north by northeast
       on the open sky road.

Acknowledgments

Gratefully acknowledged are the following publications, in which particular poems were first published in earlier versions:

"Art & Mathematics" — *Commonweal*
"At the End of the Day" — *Commonweal*
"August, the Wee Hours" — *egg*
"Black and Red and Blue on White, 2022" — *Oberon*
"A Bridge Not High Enough" — *The Midwest Quarterly*
"The Colors of Desire" — *The Linnet's Wings*
"Coming Back" — *The Lake*
"Defining Ourselves" — *Cultural Weekly*
"The Dirt" — *Commonweal*
"Dreaming Awake" — *The Lake*
"Eudora Welty Writes a Story" — *The Maine Review*
"Fire Season" — *California Fire & Water: A Climate Crisis Anthology*
"The First Day, King James Version, Revised" — *Cloudbank*
"Flight Plan" first appeared in *Cultural Weekly* (*Cultural Daily*)
"Here and There" — *The Lake*
"In Sheep's Clothing" — *The Squaw Valley Review*
"The Innocents" — *The Inflectionist Review*
"Inside a Pearl" — *Commonweal*
"Just Because I Can" — *Epoch*
"Love's Latitudes" — *Fish Anthology 2022*, judged by Billy Collins
"Lower Mathematics" — *Commonweal*
"Not the End of the World" — *New World Writing*
"One Early-Summer Day, Looking Back" — *Written Here & There*
"The Other Heaven" — *Commonweal*
"Paper Wings" — *The MacGuffin*

"The Places Between" — *Catamaran*
"Prairie Prom" first appeared in *Postcard Poems and Prose*
"Reading the Night" — *Sylvia*
"Rending Flesh" — *Wisconsin Review*
"Sky Writing" — *Miramar*
"The Speed of Firelight" — *New World Writing*
"Supermoon Night" — *Tule Review*
"Syzygy: The Full Long Nights Moon" — *The Inflectionist Review*
"Time to Murder and Create" — *burntdistrict*
"To the Boy, To the Dog, To the Farmer" — *Innisfree Poetry Journal*
"Watching the Sky" — *Oberon*
"While She's Thinking About Weeks of Bad News" — *The Inflectionist Review*
"The Woman on C Street (or D Street)" — *The MacGuffin*
"Zero in Kyiv" — *egg*

The following appeared in *Flat Water: Nebraska Poems* (Judy Brackett Crowe; Finishing Line Press 2019):

"Flight Plan"
"Geography of a Cloud"
"Prairie Prom"

Gratefully acknowledged are the following contests, where poems from this collection received recognition:

Oberon Poetry Prize, 1st place, *Oberon Twentieth* Annual Issue 2022
The Fish Poetry Prize, 2nd place, *Fish Anthology* 2022 (Billy Collins, judge)
The MacGuffin Poet Hunt Contest, grand prize, *The MacGuffin*, Winter 2023

Thank you to everyone at Cornerstone Press, especially Dr. Ross Tangedal, Brett Hill, Kirsten Faulkner, Grace Dahl, Carolyn Czerwinski, Ava Willett, Sophie McPherson, and Natalie Reiter. And thank you to Beth C. Ford (once again) for a beautiful cover.

I have many to thank for support, encouragement, and friendship. Thank you to the Community of Writers; the Kimmel Harding Center for the Arts in Nebraska City; the Anam Cara Writer's and Artist's

Retreat in Eyeries, County Cork, Ireland; and to the legions of inspiring and unsung English teachers., with a nod to the memory of Kathryn "Kay" Martin.

Thank you to friends—poets and writers, book friends, walking-and-talking friends—Karla Arens, Linda Baran, Gene Berson, Gretchen Bond, Kirsten Casey, Julie Cobden, Mary Crowe, Marilyn Darlington, Susan Duey, Charles Entrekin, Gail Entrekin, Molly Fisk, Beth Ford, Sands Hall, Lynn Johnson, Brett Hall Jones, Maxima Kahn, Joan Keyes, Jenny Long, JoAnn Marie, Patricia McLean, Patricia Miller, Judie Rae, Sharon Richardson, Diane Robertson, Julie Valin, and many others. And thank you to my siblings—Brenda, Devra, David, and Pam.

Thank you, always, to my family—Jeanne-Marie and Don, Esther Rose, Quinn; Jonathan and Christi, Finnegan; Matthew, Jack and Brie, Sam.

Judy Brackett Crowe's stories and poems have appeared in many literary journals and anthologies. She is the author of *Flat Water: Nebraska Poems* (2019) and a member of the Community of Writers. Born in Nebraska, she's lived in a small town in the northern Sierra Nevada foothills of California for many years.

www.ingramcontent.com/pod-product-compliance
Lightning Source LLC
Chambersburg PA
CBHW031428120626
46545CB00006B/2311